Standard: average or normal, common. The Standard Poodle
 is anything but standard. It is a standout as one of the most
utility breeds; they can do it all. Even though all Standards
are outstanding; each and every one is an individual.

The standard poodle is the largest of the poodles; standing
over 15 inches at the withers and is an extremely athletic dog.
As an enthusiastic athlete the Standard Poodle is typically up
for any sport you'd like to give a try. Many are highly
driven with an amazing work ethic.

The Standard poodle is highly intelligent; often easily
outsmarting their owners.   Their ability to understand
and perform day to day tasks is uncanny as is there
clear comprehension of our vocabulary.

The Standard Poodle

Color: The standard poodle comes in just about every color that you can imagine. Not all Kennel Clubs recognize all colors. Depending on where you are located in the world and what Kennel Club you are registered with will factor greatly in what is a recognized color.   Of course this is only of concern if you intend on showing your dog. I think that all of the colors, mix of colors and patterns are fabulous.

There is truly a plethora of colors to choose from. Black, white, all of the spectrum of browns, silver, blue, gray, apricot, cream and reds. They come in combinations as well. The whole range of colors combined to make the parti, phantom, sable and multi-patterned. No matter what color a Standard Poodle is; it is a Standard Poodle.

Who's in the book? Have a look.

There are four sections within the book.

The Standard Poodle
Babies
Those Beautiful Faces
Athletes

Cover - Abby

JORDI AND ELLIE

STAR

JEDI

SOPHIE AND CASS

GRACIE AND ALEXA

HANK

RUFUS AND EMMA

DIVA

RITA

BOB

SOPHIE

ZOE

MAGIC

LUKE

ELI

LONDON

STELLA

JIMMY

MOCHA

BOB

BLAZE AND TERRA

LUKE

UNO

PUPPIES - IS THERE ANYTHING CUTER THAN A BABY STANDARD POODLE?

ESPREE puppies

DESERT REEF puppy

BROOK

AMMALIANTE RED STANDARDS puppies

DE BERGERAC puppies

SHORELINE puppies

AMMALIANTE RED STANDARDS puppy

BROOK

ESPREE puppy

DE BERGERAC puppy

AMMALIANTE RED STANDARDS puppy

MISCHA

ELSA

CLEO

ESPREE puppy

NICKY

MARIAH

DE BERGERAC puppies

MISCHA

ESPREE puppies

HANK

ESPREE puppy

ESPREE puppy

DESERT REEF puppies

ELSA

THOSE BEAUTIFUL FACES

CoCo

JAVA

CHARISSE

LIBOR

LONDON

RAGZZ

RUBY

ELSA

TILLEY

ANGIE

HANK

DELANEY

POP

ROJO

SHEIMA

NALA

UNO

ZYAN

SUZY

AMBER

KATIE

MJ

CHELSIE

LUKE

SHANTI

ATHLETES -

Non-sporting group?

Ya right!!!

PHEOBE

MANGO

CHELSIE

SASSY

CHARISSE

TILLEY

CoCo

TILLEY AND LUKE

CASS

SHASTA

RUFUS

GLORIA

SALLY

ROJO

BUNNY

WINNIE

SALLY

ABBY

TILLEY

JOHANN

WOLFGANG

Quotes from a few Standard Poodle lovers

Zydeco and Zulu are the perfect beginning and ending to every day. Unconditional love always! Elisa Young Cole

I always say that my standard poodle is "Legally Blonde smart". She could pass Harvard with no problem but that's not going to stop her from tripping over her own feet or running into the sliding glass door. Amber Jarrett

Dolly (Dollywog) is my best friend. She is comfortable just hanging out, chasing critters, staying in nice hotels or going for a ride up the driveway when Dad gets home from work. Dona Mastin

Jessica chose me and battled the odds to be mine, in the process of her living, she taught me and all who met her, the truest things of love and grace. Charlotte V Cobb (Mommie)

Lichen makes my heart sing with the warmth of his eyes, intelligence, humor, personality and movement. He is just a being of beauty. Adrienne Bea Smith

"I didn't know love until I was loved by a poodle. I would spend every moment of every day with my Paisley if I could." CES

" I have two...It's like living with two 4 legged humans.
They are complex, intuitive, crazy and fun all in one curly package."
LS-laguna beach

"Radio is the patient observer. He seems aloof, but he has his paw on the pulse of what is going on. Kaizen oozes oodles and oodles of love and affection from every wiggly, giggly fiber of her being." Christy Knight

"My boy, Jedi, put the Vel in Velcro Dog! If he ventures even an inch from my side, I swear I can hear that Velcro sound!!" Kathie Taylor

"In 50 years of being owned by Poodles, I have never known a dog more filled with joy in just being alive as Quincy. He is my heart!" Cherie Perks

"A dog with a sense of humor – who knew?? Franklin makes us smile and laugh daily." Rachel and Jeff Fogle, Norwich, CT

"I have never known a doggie that loves people (or a camera) more than Sheima. "Miss Personality" has introduced me to many nice people who have become the best of friends. Thank you, girlfriend, for enriching my life!"
Lynn Meade

"Maggie and Maverick inspire me everyday to put a little "spring" in my step. If attitude is half the battle - they've got that half "licked."" Christina Madden

"Luke and Elsa are my constant and highly intelligent companions. Whether I'm working in the office, hiking, baking or gardening; they are by my side. They bring me great joy by simply being Luke and Elsa." Sherri Regalbuto

ELSA

ANDRE

HANK

CHARISSE AND JOSEPHINE

DILLON

The Many Talents Of The Standard Poodle

Never underestimate the extreme intelligence, amazing athletism, sheer strength, drive or determination of a Standard Poodle. They are an amazing breed of dog; capable of anything they or you set a mind to. They excel in the obedience ring, agility, herding, hunting, frisbee, search and rescue, seeing eye, service, dock diving, lure coursing, scent work, flyball and the therapy field.

There really isn't anything that The Standard Poodle cannot do.

Made in the USA
Middletown, DE
24 October 2023

41333040R00062